Stories of Food and Life

A voyage to culinary pleasure by the scenic route

by Mariuccia Milla

Author of

Meet Me in Milano

Blue Sky with Clouds

The Audiobook, "Stories of Food and Life" is narrated by

Dr. Sandra Boysen Sluberski of SBS Vocalworx

and produced by

Dave Sluberski of West Rush Media.

Illustrations by **Penelope Spica**.

Cover design by Pebble-stream.

Thank You

to my Kickstarter campaign donors

with a special mention to:

Carla Dannels

Christina Marketos

Robert Miller

Oksana Miller

Arturo Spica

Penelope Spica

and

In honor of strong women who never, never, never, never give up.

Table of Contents

1. Penne all'arrabbiata

The road to Ludovico's house was not a crushed stone drive that wound up a Tuscan hill accompanied by cypresses. You know, the kind silhouetted against the sunset on the cover of romantic novels in the "Italy porn" genre.

Instead, it was a narrow alley whose masonry buildings stood at point blank with the edges of a street where pedestrians scattered only slowly, like jaded farmyard chickens. We were driving a red Fiat Cinquecento, thankfully, and deftly made the tight turn through the arched portal that led into the cobblestone courtyard. The Milanese fog had lifted and the sun was starting to appear, white and diffuse, through the gauzy air. The gray of everything was offset by the red car and the ochre-tinted plaster of the building chipped in some spots.

Ludovico had an American visitor named Roberto who had recently arrived from a place called Watkins Glen. He was preparing lunch. I was visiting Milan from the Ligurian town of Camogli, where I had spent the summer rehabilitating a private garden that had fallen into disarray. Ludo's partner, Alessandra, was my host in Milan; she had invited me to tag along.

I had been going back and forth between Italy and the U.S., and while I did meet some expats during my stays in the *bel paese*, I generally avoided other Americans. I didn't think we had much in common.

Ludovico's apartment was a third-floor walk-up with windows on both the courtyard as well as the canal. He greeted us enthusiastically in the foyer, while his guest held back. I walked down the short corridor to the kitchen. Roberto was tying an apron at his back.

"The first thing is to pour a glass of wine," he said after I introduced myself.

Roberto's blue eyes had nothing of the pretty boy about them thanks to his luxuriously bushy black eyebrows. The eyes themselves were penetrating, searching, and a little careworn. He looked to me like someone who was missing something longed-for in his life. Yet he was happily preparing our lunch of *penne all'arrabbiata*. The tools were arrayed, the wine was airing, and he held a bulb of garlic in his right hand, which he set on the counter so that he could shake mine.

"Why do you go by Roberto," I asked, "and not Robert?"

"It is Robert," he said, "but Ludovico has decided to Italianize my name. He doesn't like it when people call me 'Bohb.'"

"Okay, Roberto," I conceded. "Thank you for making our lunch."

"I like to make people happy," he said. "Especially when I'm here because Italians enjoy food more than Americans do."

"Americans like to eat, by the looks of things," Alessandra said.

"Overeating or depriving ourselves, that's what we do," I said.

"Exactly," said Roberto. "The U.S. is still a Puritan country at heart. Sin and repentance."

He poured some extra-virgin olive oil into a skillet and started peeling garlic cloves with a small knife.

"I'm generally not very good at enjoying things I have to do," Roberto said to me, "but I seemed to have managed it with cooking."

"What brings you to Italy?" I asked him.

"It suits me," he answered. "I love the food, the wine, the cars, and the countryside. And the people, of course! I met Ludovico through a mutual friend on my last visit. He invited me to stay for a few days here before I head to Montepulciano. I'm taking a full-immersion course in Italian next week."

Roberto had plucked the leaves from a bunch of fresh parsley and placed them in a small drinking glass. He took the kitchen scissors and started snipping the leaves in the glass.

"Why do you that?" I asked.

"The parsley is confined in the glass, and that makes it easier to cut," he said.

By now the garlic was getting *abbrustolito*, or toasted, an even brown. Roberto carefully picked the cloves out one at a time and placed them in a small bowl. Then he tossed hot pepper flakes, or *peperoncino*, into the oil, and I watched them skitter at a respectful distance. The pungency filled the small kitchen, drifting up my nostrils. It made my eyes water.

"Toasting the garlic and the *peperoncino* is what gives the sauce its flavor," said Roberto.

"It puts the *rabbia* into *all'arrabbiata*," Ludovico said, filling a pot with water from the sink.

"You're using canned tomatoes," said Alessandra.

"Yes, well, that's my habit in the States, because I like to use Italian tomatoes. The soil is different, and you can taste it in the tomatoes. Besides, if I used fresh tomatoes, it would take too long for lunch. I'd have to remove the skins. This sauce is more spontaneous than ritualistic to me."

"Well," said Alessandra, taking a sip of wine, "I don't have to agree with you to recognize that it is very Italian to have an opinion about cooking. We'll have to make you an honorary citizen."

He lowered the heat and dumped the diced tomatoes into the skillet, standing back to avoid the fallout.

"Where are you staying in Montepulciano?" I asked.

"In an *osteria* that has rooms for the students," he answered, then asked me, "What brings you to Italy?"

"I used to live here. Then, I went back to the U.S. But I never really settled back into it. I think that once you're an expat, you kind of lose your original nationality without gaining a new one. You're in expat limbo forever."

"I know what you mean," he said. He looked at me with his penetrating eyes. That was where he smiled, rather than with his mouth. I had trouble returning his gaze. It was as if he wanted to unlock my secrets, and it made me feel vulnerable. I just looked down.

The aroma of the sauce permeated the room. I wanted to grab a piece of bread and dip it into the simmering red tomatoes. Roberto fingered through Ludo's utensils until he found a potato masher, then gently pressed the diced tomatoes, now softening, in the skillet.

"Now I need to grate some parmigiano," he said.

The sharp odor of the cheese introduced itself into the bouquet, like the bright and unexpected sound of the triangle in an orchestra.

"You must be a good listener," I said to Roberto.

"Why do you say that?" he asked.

"Because you use all of your senses when you're cooking."

He looked at me askance, with his head down and his eyes smiling again. When I returned his gaze this time, he raised his luxurious eyebrows in some sort of a challenge.

I liked this Roberto, although he was very different from anyone I had previously met. He wasn't like an Italian guy, with their romantic subterfuge. And he was nothing like an American. He lacked the American prejudice about the world; he had understood our nation, as I did, from the outside looking in.

Like me, he was a natural-born expatriate.

This was both a welcome and frustrating revelation for the simple reason that he was out of my league. He was too good-looking to pay attention to someone like me.

He dumped a handful of salt and a box of *penne rigate* into the boiling water. Then he looked up at me.

"Is Montepulciano very far from where you're staying in Liguria?"

"Far meaning too far to travel for a lark?" I asked.

"No, I mean, too far to travel to be my guest for the weekend."

I was unable to respond, not sure of what he meant. Alessandra came back into the kitchen from setting the table.

"You can take the Super Rapido train to Florence," she said to me, popping an olive into her mouth.

"Well," Roberto said, "I'm going back tomorrow, and if you can make it, I'd love to take you to dinner on Saturday."

Alessandra looked at him, then at me, and said, "Of course she'll come."

I glared at her while Roberto drained the pasta into a colander in the sink.

He put a little bit of raw olive oil on the pasta in the serving bowl before mixing in the sauce. He looked at the three of us anticipating our meal and decided to try out his Italian.

"*La pasta é pronta!*" he said.

Lunch was ready.

2. La bruschetta (or, Too Hot to Shop)

By the time we reached Ginevra's rustic little house, I was truly travel-worn.

My hair was stuck to the back of my neck, which was itself stiff from the flight. My clothes were rumpled. My left ear had not yet recovered from having popped during the descent. My feet were swollen.

The last piece of road was short and very steep, yet Ginevra managed to navigate it with ease, even making a ninety-degree turn onto the gravel strip in her yard where she kept her car. We passed through the garden, ascended a flight of stairs, crossed a cart path, and entered her house, which was as cool as a cave. Ginevra began the ritual of opening the windows and pulling in the green-painted shutters, latching them so that they were slightly ajar.

There we were: two sisters, licking our wounds from our failed relationships in a tiny hill town above the Italian Riviera. Once I had caught up on my sleep, we settled into the meditation of our daily routine. Every morning we got up and opened the shutters one by one, fastening them to the outside of the thick masonry walls. We had an espresso and a small, plain cookie; our injection of caffeine and sugar. Then we made the beds and put in the laundry. On those hot, sunny days in the hills above the sea, our wardrobe consisted of simple dresses and sandals. Pull it over your head and done!

We grabbed our bags and hopped on Ginevra's scooter. She drove like an expert down the steep hills, around the tight curves, and along the narrow roads bordered by stone walls. We shared a running commentary on the sights and the locals as we descended into Rapallo and made our rounds among the shops. Then we returned up the hills, around the curves, and between the stone walls, this time laden with four or five bags stuffed between our legs or hanging from the handgrips. But Ginevra got up the last stretch despite our burden.

While down in Rapallo we reflected on the betrayals we had experienced, whether of faith or in deed, and the way we responded to them, over a cappuccino and a brioche. We walked the promenade along the shore of the Mediterranean, where North African migrants sold trinkets, and elderly couples sat on benches under palm trees. Children carefully scrambled among the boulders that formed the sea wall.

When we unpacked the focaccia and the rest of the food, we unloaded the wash into a plastic tub and carried it across the cart path onto a narrow strip of land above the *casetta* that served as a writer's cottage in Ginevra's garden. That was where the clothesline was strung.

There is such an elemental and beautiful craft to the act of hanging clothes on a line: the spacing, the folding over of the collars, the strategic positioning of the pins so that they hold the clothing firmly though gingerly; and the occasional overlap of shirts when lack of line required.

The breeze coming up the hill draped us with the damp cloth of the clothes as we worked. The cicadas were waxing into a din, their song dominating our consciousness. The garden below was dusty, with its scattered olive trees and lemon trees and the laurel hedge, though there was no lawn to speak of. A wooden platform the size of a living room held furniture with faded cushions strewn with fallen twigs. We went down to the long table under the pergola, a table with a thin and worn marble top set on an iron frame. There was a utility sink where we washed the arugula and the plums. Our mozzarella, dribbled with olive oil and sprinkled with black pepper, was arranged on an oval platter. We drank chilled white wine from the Cinque Terre. I looked up at the house, a small, simple, and beautiful thing, up the stairs and across the cart path. It was attached to another dwelling, delineated by the sudden end of the white stucco on the rough walls. The neighbor's garden was alongside their place, on the terrace above where we sat. Chickens wandered within the wire fencing that was anchored to the stone retaining walls above the cart path. We would see those birds prancing with their bobbing heads whenever we passed behind the houses during our walks along the ridge.

After we had lunched and lamented further about our exes, sometimes mocking, sometimes laughing, sometimes with the wipe of a tear from the corner of an eye, we went inside to the cool cave and lay down to rest through the heat of the afternoon.

Later in the day, when the tourists had retreated and the locals had retaken possession of the stony beaches and hidden coves, we would go down to the sea to swim. We splashed around or snorkeled, depending on whether we walked into shallow water or slipped into the sea from a rocky promontory. Sometimes we climbed out, nicking our knees, sometimes even stung by a jellyfish.

When we were somewhat drier, and the sun had started to sink, we'd make our way uphill–always up, up, up, whether by stairs or a winding path–and have an *aperitivo* at a bar carved out of a hillside or projecting from a stony cliff. We sipped Negronis and nibbled on tiny pieces of focaccia and olives.

Our condition was a perfect combination of nature and nurture. There was the boundless sea, pushing and pulling, gathering our worries and hurt and dragging them off to dispose of them on some faraway, deserted beach. We also had each other, and the secret language of sisters, where a raised eyebrow or a catalogued phrase was enough to ensure complete comprehension.

By and by, a salty crust made our skin feel tight and that, together with our guilt about over-snacking, sent us back up the hills, around the curves, and between the stone walls to Ginevra's garden. We rinsed off in the outdoor shower tucked under the wall, out of view, and changed into some fresh clothes. Then Ginevra put some water on for pasta while I removed the clothes from the line before the evening's saline humidity got the better of them.

Our meal was simple, and when we finished, we locked the shutters and closed the windows, and went to bed, talking and laughing until we fell asleep.

Something was reassuring about this routine, performed day after day, under the same sunny skies, in the same warm air, with the cicadas humming like our rhythm section.

But the crescendo of yellow buzzing heat reached a high point one day so that we didn't even want to go down into town for our cappuccino and brioche.

It was too hot to shop!

We closed the shutters, protecting the rooms from the sun. The neighborhood cats sought shady corners near the steps, and Ginevra put fresh water out in little bowls for them. We read and wrote and ate leftover pasta for lunch.

"You know, sis, we don't have anything for supper tonight," Ginevra said.

I sighed. "I saw that your neighbor's tomatoes have ripened nicely."

"And so?"

"Well, if they're away for the weekend, we wouldn't want them to rot on the vine, would we?"

"We're out of pasta, anyway," Ginevra noted.

"Do we have any bread?"

"From yesterday. It's a bit stale, though."

Ah, now there was the basis of a plan. And as we went to take our afternoon nap, the only sound was the deafening din of the cicadas. I couldn't sleep because my mind was on those tomatoes, and now everyone was indoors, except for the cats who slept in the shade along the cart path.

I walked around the back of the neighbor's house and along the wire fence enclosing their garden. There was a pillar in between two sections, with a few footholds where the brick had chipped, or a piece of iron hardware was exposed. I carefully climbed it, neglecting to check the other side for similar opportunities. Once around the pillar, I had to drop about four feet to the ground. As I did so, one of my buttons was caught in the fence so that I was on the ground among the eggplant and the peppers, with my dress hiked up on one side up to my butt. The ridiculousness of the situation made me laugh as I stood there, sweltering in the heat, looking for a way to free the button. But it was no use: I had to yank the dress and lose it. The button fell to the other side of the fence and rolled down the upper cart path and out of sight.

I was able to get back out of the garden by way of another pillar that was better equipped for climbing on the inside. I had a small bag with me, now containing three large, red tomatoes, which I tied to the outside of the fence as soon as I was high enough to reach over it. After I landed awkwardly on the outside, an older man with a rake and hoe over his shoulder appeared around the bend.

"*Buona sera*!" I said, acting as if it was perfectly reasonable to be outside in the heat of the day with no apparent purpose. But it was evident that he was as embarrassed as I.

"My son left the tools out again!" he complained. "Anyone could take them, with everyone sleeping."

"Quite right!" I answered. He saluted me and continued down the path, toward his stone tool shed and, probably, my lost button.

Once he was out of sight, I untied the tomatoes and went around the uphill side of the attached dwellings, down and back inside Ginevra's house. I stayed downstairs to avoid waking her, dozing intermittently on the sofa.

When dinnertime approached, I got up from my book and starting rummaging around the kitchen. The idea of roughing it appealed to me. I put a bottle of white wine in the fridge and started slicing, or rather sawing, the stale bread. Ginevra had a tiny, beat-up grill out in the garden with some half-spent charcoal in it. It was enough for *bruschetta*.

Ginevra was in the shower for the third time that day.

I arranged the slices on a metal tray. Then I poured some olive oil into a small bowl and added a clove of garlic, some *peperoncino,* and oregano, mixing it with a brush. Then I cored and chopped the tomatoes. I brought everything out to the marble table under the pergola and started the fire on the grill with some dry sticks.

"I have some starter brick thingys," said Ginevra, descending the stairs with the wine and two glasses.

"This makes it more challenging," I said. "I'm feeling primitive."

Together we moved the grill to a more tolerable spot, closer to the table, downwind, and sipped a little wine while I poked at the charcoal.

"I'll pick some arugula," Ginevra said. She went over beyond the outdoor shower to the unkempt bed where arugula and basil and rosemary grew with abandon. She washed it in the ceramic sink behind the marble table and let it drain in a colander. Then we sat down to assemble the *bruschette,* brushing each piece of bread with the oil infusion and adding the chopped tomatoes on top.

I placed them on the grill, now hot, and let the old bread get singed on the edges before I removed each piece with tongs and carried the *bruschette* back to the table.

And there we sat, with our wine, and the old, burnt bread embellished with hot flavors and sun-drenched tomatoes, feeling that we, too, had become better, annealed by fire and with our warm companionship and simple dinner, all was right in the world.

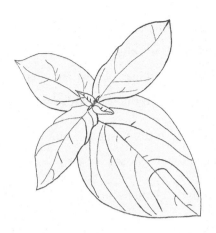

3. Trofie al pesto

I didn't know what to expect when I arrived in Italy. I was focused on what I was leaving behind, waiting for the new sights, sounds, and sensations to pour into my consciousness and displace my history, my language, and my outlook.

My second cousin, Amelia, was kind enough to offer me a place to stay in the little town of Sori in the beautiful region of Liguria. Her apartment was the upper story of an asymmetrical dwelling, each level of which was accessed from landings on a long flight of steps that started at the edge of the road. That road happened to be the Via Aurelia, one of those famous roads that led and still leads to Rome. When you reached the top of the steps, there was a garden terrace that you crossed the long way to get to a small court entry with some planting beds available for Amelia's use. Small lizards sunned on the patio stone, including an occasional victim of Amelia's kitty, who used to bat at them, swiping their tails off. When the giant and ferocious creature came near, the lizards would dart underneath the artichoke shrubs.

The balcony on the downhill side of the apartment had a full view of the sea and a bird's-eye view of the Riviera that tumbled down to it. The beach was below the Aurelia, below the pastel houses perched on the slope, below the railroad tracks and gardens and more houses, down, down to the rocky water's edge. Narrow steps descended in between the dwellings, while switchback roads provided a more passable, though still intrepid, access for vehicles.

I have a distinct memory of the sweet fragrance of the water. It would come back to me every time I visited, as soon as I opened a faucet. The trofie, the pesto, and the focaccia are the fruit of that sweet water. I've grown basil, but it has never achieved the flavor that comes from the Ligurian soil and water.

A widowed woman and her grown son inhabited the flat below. Her tireless activity could be glimpsed on the way up the steps or when watering the geraniums on the balcony that overlooked hers below. She would be there in the mornings, like clockwork, hanging washed clothes to dry while we were still dunking cookies in our caffè latte.

When we returned from the morning shopping, we could see her through the kitchen window, mixing the sweet water with a pile of the finest durum wheat semolina, working the *impasto* with her hands until she had patted it into shapes like little dolls' pillows. I set my bags on the landing to catch my breath and marvel at her craftsmanship. She would take each of these pieces of dough, or *impasto*, and work them, again with her hands, into long, slender snake-like rolls.

Then, this widowed woman took a disc-shaped tool, a piece of stone with a sharpened edge, and deftly cut the snake into half-inch pieces. She pushed them aside as she worked, sprinkling them with flour as they accumulated on her marble tabletop. Fascinated, I tried to stay out of view; for she was a dour-looking woman, all work and no joy in her life except the sight of her son gobbling her food or tucking a pressed linen shirt into his trousers.

She then took each of these now even smaller cushion shapes and set them, one at a time, on the heel of her left hand. She placed her right fingertips over it, and slid her right hand over her left, spinning the little piece, so it flew off and landed on the cool marble in its new and final form.

This hand-rubbing movement that creates the pasta is the likely source of the name "trofie." It may come from the Ligurian version of the Italian word, *strofinare*, which means, to rub. I later learned that this part of Liguria was the epicenter of trofie, even before this pasta type arrived in Genoa, where it was considered a form of gnocchi. But I don't want to get too much into the weeds here, as the Ligurians are a dying breed jealous of their culture and each one is sure to have their own version of history. The point is, the Signora had learned this technique from her mother, who had learned it from hers, and so on. It was the real deal.

When she looked up from her work, I quickly bent over to grab my bags from the greengrocer and continued up the endless flight of steps to reach Amelia's. I wondered about the Signora and what she thought about her own life. It was like that of so many Italian women living in small towns. Those of them with husbands had no advantage: their work was harder and their evenings just as lonely, given that their mates, once their bellies were full, would go off to smoke and play cards at the local bar-café.

And so, the life of these unsung heroines of the kitchens and the gardens and the polished floors was a litany of chores, each in their allotted timeframe and according to weather and season, making of their days a meditation as rhythmic as the tides of the sea. Just as their lives frightened me, I recognized their role as guardians of cultural gestures and words and flavors that are now awash with globalization and misappropriation by superficial consumers of culture.

The Signora made her pesto after she had finished rotating her clothing on the drying rack. She used a mortar and pestle (hence the name *pesto*) made of the same Carrara marble as her kitchen tabletop. I know this because she had laid her basil on a kitchen cloth on her balcony and used the mortar to hold down the fabric while she entered her kitchen to collect the pine nuts and garlic.

I was snipping the dried leaves on the geraniums when I called down to her.

"Buongiorno, Signora, che profumo!" I said. *What an aroma!*

Amelia glared at me for the liberty I had taken with her stoic neighbor. And rightly so, as the Signora looked up at me and drew her mouth into a straight line, perturbed by this foreign girl who had made her miss a beat. You just didn't do things like that here.

She wasn't the type to prepare food outside, but I suspect that my attempt to be friendly, as well as the pleasant breeze coming in from the sea, led her to work within my view so that if I stood in a specific position, I could observe without her acknowledging it.

She scooped up the basil leaves and put them into the mortar, covering a clove of garlic on the bottom. Then she added the pine nuts, which made it easier to crush the basil under the pestle. Her arms were strong from hanging clothes and polishing floors and the ironing she did every day before her son's shirts were completely dry.

It is believed that the Ligurians used *fiore sardo*, or Sardinian pecorino cheese, rather than parmigiano because they had interacted less with the rest of the Italian peninsula than with the people and places of their corner of the Mediterranean, shared with the islands and the Riviera of France. She may have also insisted on Ligurian olive oil, although I will never know because she ducked inside before adding the final ingredients.

I went inside and started plucking some basil leaves myself. Being less orthodox, I allowed myself Tuscan oil, parmigiano cheese, and store-bought pasta. I'm intent on learning how to make trofie and pesto the traditional way, but for today I'll layer basil, garlic, toasted pine nuts and chips of parmigiano into a food processor for a first round before adding the extra-virgin olive oil. I know, I'm a Philistine, but I come from a generation that snubs the household activities relegated to women so that we can function in more powerless roles in offices, without polished floors.

So, we gain something, and we lose something, just like the sea each time it rolls into the shore and recedes once again.

4. Il fico (The Fig Tree)

We bought the abandoned farmhouse, and it would have been against our better judgment, had we had any ability to judge. We could have merely insulated and heated it, perhaps installed new windows, but each intervention had a domino effect: before we knew it, we were digging below grade and removing the walls and roof, literally rebuilding the whole 4,000 square foot structure on the original framework.

The house was on a few acres of land in a nondescript rural town fifteen-minutes south of Lago Maggiore and one hour's drive from Milan. The garden wrapped around the house in an "L" and the fig tree was in the crook, backdropped by our neighbor's masonry outbuilding and visible from every angle, thanks to the complementary L-shape of our house. Our upper floors had exterior walkways ringed with wrought iron rails. The rooms along the walkway had French doors, allowing ample opportunity to survey our simple country garden from above.

My good friend Marino, who as a boy stole food from Nazi soldiers to survive, was a *contadino* and now grew his own vegetables and fruit. He worked as a gardener for others and so helped me to plant shrubs and advised me on small food crops. He was very orderly, as most people engaged in plant husbandry are. He once brought me a crate of kiwis picked from his pergola, each piece of fruit perfectly aligned so that it resembled a box of hand grenades. It was with this attention to detail that he pruned our fig tree.

Now, if you have never witnessed the Italian pruning technique, let me say that it can be quite shocking; they cut with confidence. I was afraid we'd never see the tree flourish again, but Marino was as right about this as he was about everything else when it came to plants and grappa.

That tree, with its muscular limbs and coarse-textured leaves, lorded over a small patch of hydrangeas whose white flowerheads, because of the natural mulch of the fig droppings, displayed a succession of color splotches in every spectacular shade from green to pink to purple as the season progressed. We couldn't harvest the figs fast enough, so the shrubs shared in the bounty.

We used to shop at the markets every day with our two small children, migrating from Oleggio on Monday to Sesto Calende on Wednesday and Arona on Thursday. There, we'd meet friends at a café and have a cappuccino while the children charmed the other patrons or ran around in the piazza near our outdoor table. We'd buy fresh bread and cheese, and the *salumiere* would slice a piece of prosciutto for our son, Jacopo.

Then we would return home to the litany of our daily activities: Piero in his studio, painting; Jacopo, hard at play with Legos; and Pinuccia, torturing the cats. Both children wandered into the garden now and then, picking chives and anything else they recognized as food to snack on. My job was managing everything.

At one point, I decided we needed a frog pond. I hired someone with a backhoe to dig a rough twelve-by-eight-foot oval about two feet deep in the center. Then Marino and I refined the shape and put in the liner, tucking it under the soil.

I asked Marino how to get frogs for the pond.

"Don't worry," he said, "they'll find it."

I couldn't believe that frogs would magically arrive when there were no other ponds in the area. So, I decided to go to an aquatic plant nursery, where the owners were happy to allow me to scoop some polliwogs, of which they had an abundant supply.

I carefully conveyed my bucket home and poured its contents into the now-filled pond.

Jacopo watched from his perch in the fig tree. Its branchlets had sprouted, the fruits were forming, and by the time the large-lobed leaves filled out the crown, both Jacopo and Pinuccia treated it as their private fort. Its thick branches provided a comfortable saddle at a manageable height from the ground. They spent a lot of time there, doing nothing, just being kids in their kids' world.

The Fig, a member of the Mulberry family, is a native of the Middle East and Western Asia. It isn't hard to imagine how it migrated to Italy and spread through the Mediterranean as far as Portugal. The Romans likely had an essential role in this. It is believed that the Fig is one of the earliest plants intentionally cultivated.

Fig fruits contain flowers turned outside-in: in the case of wild figs, specialized wasps would enter them through an opening and pollinate them during their life cycle. This is why the fruit has persisted as a symbol of female reproductive organs.

Italian immigrants, always looking for a piece of land to grow food crops, brought Fig saplings and planted them throughout New York, especially in Brooklyn. It was discovered, however, that California was the ideal place to cultivate figs, and so they were introduced there, with many experiments made in species selection and pollination techniques since the days of the Gold Rush.

Figs can have two crops per year, but our fig tree produced its blue-violet fruit in September, and in Italy, these are called *settembrini*. During our last September at that country house, we had a bumper crop. My friends urged me to make preserves, but that was more than I could handle, especially since I am not fond of sugar.

As a compromise, we decided to have a dinner party and invited our friends from the surrounding towns to join us. What could we do with the figs?

That morning we had purchased four loaves of fresh bread, and I decided to get a block of the best Danish butter, just in case. Our friend Marco, the son of the *salumiere*, offered to bring us some *prosciutto di Parma* from their most prized cut. Now an idea was beginning to form in my head.

I instructed Jacopo to pick the softest, ripest figs from the tree, while Pinuccia stood underneath, collecting the occasionally dropped fruit, squishing it open and taking a bite of the soft flesh before dropping it under the hydrangeas.

Once we had all the ingredients assembled, the four of us sat along the ten-foot-long dining table made of timbers we recovered from the original structure of our house. That was our social altar, the place where we gathered with our friends to eat, drink, and sing along to the strumming of guitars.

Piero was assigned the job of slicing the bread on the diagonal. Then he passed the pieces to Jacopo to arrange in stacks. After that, the two of them carefully spread the Danish butter over the entire surface of each slice. My job was next: with a fine-tined fork, I carefully separated each thin piece of prosciutto and laid it over the buttered bread, folding it back and forth again so that it would fit neatly. Then Pinuccia would press on the figs, one by one, splitting them open and smearing their innards on top of the prosciutto. Piero and Jacopo took her work and arranged the pieces on trays, after which Jacopo ground black pepper on top.

In the end, our guests wanted nothing more than to feast on these appetizers and chase them with the lively and young red wine that our friend Ugo had purchased in the Piedmont region and bottled himself under the auspices of the correct phase of the moon. However, dinner did follow, along with the singing, until the children were sliding off their seats and had to be hauled to bed.

The next day I went out to the pond to see if I could find any polliwogs swimming around. I bent very close to the bank plantings but could not discern any. Just then, something leaped from the grass and plof! A full-grown frog landed on a lily pad. It had arrived by itself.

Marino, as usual, was right.

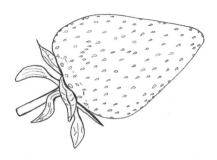

5. Risotto alle fragole (Strawberry Risotto)

The first time I had *risotto alle fragole* was at a wedding. The marriage was between the brother of a good friend of mine and a woman named Michela who, several years prior, had given birth to a baby girl. The child was the fruit of a former, casual relationship between the bride and groom during which Michela decided she wanted a baby and asked for no involvement from the father.

During her pregnancy, she started dating a certain Peter, a German expat, and fellow architect. Michela had a way of getting men to do things for her though she was neither beautiful nor particularly intelligent. She was, however, astute and gave off a libertine hippy vibe that drew men into her circle of control.

The setting for the wedding was in the industrial outskirts of Milan. Some small-scale, successful Lombard manufacturers of post-World War II vintage, now in their second or third generation, held business properties on site with their residences. I found these odd places, because their exteriors were typically plain, stuccoed concrete with barred windows and paneled metal gates that allowed no view to the interior. Inside the courtyard, you might find a fleet of company vehicles, a private gas pump, a beautiful garden, and a home stocked with valuable Modernist paintings. These were well-kept secrets, and these families were a different strain from the big money clans with their real estate in the sweet spot of Milan's center. But these small industries and their gentry were not uncommon in the outlying towns.

In the case of Michela's family, there was an artist's studio for her mother, an amateur, that Michela ostensibly designed. According to the gossip at the wedding, Peter had done the heavy lifting for the project while Michela twirled her hair and said, "I dunno, what do you think about this detail," or, "I like that idea because it fits my overall vision for the space." Peter was there for all of it, including the birth of the baby girl. He helped care for her and stayed by Michela's side until her future groom's curiosity got the better of him and he came to see his daughter. Even his mother couldn't deny her son's paternity once she had a look at her two-year-old granddaughter.

"Get married," she had said. "For the child's sake."

Food is deeply rooted in our memories. Or, are our memories rooted in food?

When I think of strawberry risotto, I remember that day touring the studio and the garden. I also remember that the risotto was like glue. This is not surprising; risotto is among the most sensitive of dishes. Attempting to serve it to one hundred and fifty people outdoors in the summertime was probably a bit too ambitious. Just the same, I associate it with Michela's wedding and her impish daughter, the real center of attention that day.

Back home in the rural town where we rented a small house, I often walked into the village center with my three-year-old, Jacopo, taking him to preschool, or going to one of the shops. We often stopped along the way to talk with our neighbors, and one day we saw our friend Ugo working in his strawberry patch.

Strawberries also have a special place in my emotional memory because they were a favorite of my mother's. She grew them under the foundation planting at our house, and I used to steal some of the berries as they ripened in June. Mom also loved strawberry milkshakes, and that was the last thing we tried to feed her after a severe stroke took her. She could still understand me when I asked if she'd like to have one. I left the hospital and went to an old-fashioned diner and placed the order; then back to the hospital. My mother couldn't muster the control to sip the strawberry milkshake, and barely uttered the words, "would like to."

Memories.

Ugo taught me that strawberry plants need plenty of space. His new plants were two feet apart, and the rows spaced at four feet. But his older plants were much denser. He explained how they propagate through runners, and that to reinvigorate the planting, he would remove the *madre*, or mother plant, after the runners that had rooted the previous year produced fruit. But this year, his patch had about five plants every square foot and a bumper crop of strawberries. I left with a small basketful, evading Jacopo's little fingers on the way home.

I resorted to what I call my conceptual understanding of Italian cooking to devise my own approach for *risotto alle fragole*. I'm not very good at following recipes; I'm more spontaneous in the kitchen. That doesn't mean I don't subscribe to the golden rule that dictates: simple treatment of the best ingredients.

That means, unfortunately, that one must only prepare *risotto alle fragole* when fresh berries are available: in our case, June. I admit that strawberries can be had all year, including frozen, organic ones. But there is a seasonal rhythm to fruits and vegetables that risks getting lost through the globalization of food distribution. We have evolved together with our local food sources, and it makes tremendous sense to go with this seasonal flow. There are reasons that we should eat things at their peak, and I believe those reasons are more complex than we can understand. There is a certain greediness in wanting everything all the time. Besides that, limited availability makes dishes more special, and they become the celebration of a fleeting moment.

In the U.S., you often see gigantic strawberries that are all lumpy. I prefer using the smaller, heart-shaped fruits that are red through to the middle. These are usually sold in pressed cardboard pints. You will see them out at the market for anywhere from a week to one month, depending on the weather. It's always a good idea to keep them out of the fridge and on the window sill, well-aerated and clean to ripen and sweeten. I like them to capture the warmth of the sun.

In this dish, the companion of the strawberry is the onion. Fortunately, fresh, sweet onions are also available at the same time, and my preferred type is the Vidalia onion, whose season is longer but overlaps that of June-bearing strawberries. I cut the onions into quarters, then slice them finely. I don't like them minced, and since they will nearly dissolve, it's not necessary.

Onions love being simmered in butter, but extra-virgin olive oil can be used or, as a compromise, a mixture of the two. Never sauté the onions on high heat; start them at a temperature that can be maintained until the onion melts in your mouth.

Another reason that Michela served strawberry risotto at her wedding was that it calls for sparkling wine, spumante, or champagne, for the deglazing. Now, this puts another constraint on when you can serve *risotto alle fragole*. Ideally, you'll have a half-empty bottle of spumante from last night in the fridge with a spoon in the neck to keep it from getting flat. It's rather extravagant to buy a bottle of bubbly to make the risotto unless you're dining with close friends, in which case you can have a toast in the kitchen during preparation.

By the time the onions have cooked sufficiently, you may be a little lightheaded. But this is the time to stay alert: you'll be adding the carnaroli rice, and you have to keep it moving while it toasts in the sauté. Keep the sparkling wine handy in case you need to cool it down. The purpose of this searing is to prevent the rice from overcooking. That is risotto suicide.

Many people use arborio rice, but my ex-mother-in-law, who was Milanese by adoption, insists that carnaroli is the way to go. It provides a creamier texture and is less likely to overcook.

By the time you're ready to add the broth, you will have used about three-quarters of a cup of wine. This is based on one cup of rice, which is enough for two to four people, depending on whether the risotto is a first or only course. The broth should be added with a ladle gradually, so you don't have a swamp when the rice is cooked. Sorry, you can't go sit in the living room. This is where you discover who your real friends are: they'll stay with you in the kitchen.

The broth is usually made from beef or chicken, but I think that is too much for this risotto. I prefer making it by simmering parmigiano rinds and a chunk of the same onion, possibly a sprig of rosemary. You should start the broth a few hours before you make the risotto, using filtered water. If you include rosemary, put it in after the boiling, when the broth is simmering, and keep it covered. Next time I make it, I am going to try lavender because I have plenty of it in my garden.

What about the strawberries? If you have nice ripe ones that are red all the way through (and you should), cut them into quarters and put them into the risotto just long enough to get to temperature, near the end.

When the rice is *al dente*, which you can only know by tasting a few grains now and then, get it off the heat right away. I personally like to take it off the burner a minute ahead of time.

The final touch is the cheese: the classic for most risottos is parmigiano, but for this one, you should use a dollop of Crescenza if you can find it. This is a soft cheese typical of Lombardy, which is the motherland of risotto. As a very last resort, you can use cream cheese, or as the Italians call it, Philadelphia.

One last thing: make sure your guests are seated at the table and ready *before* you plate the risotto.

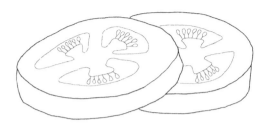

6. L'insalata Caprese (Caprese salad, or La Caprese)

Spoiler alert: there is no balsamic vinegar on the Caprese salad, not drizzled, not drazzled, it doesn't belong in this salad.

I think we tend to overcomplicate things trying to improve on perfection, especially in the U.S., where more is often considered better. To understand Italian cuisine, you have to step out into the garden, pick a ripe tomato while it's still warm from the sun, bring it into the kitchen, slice it, put a little salt on it, and eat it. Italians handle their vegetables like Native Americans treated their kill: with respect and a proper funeral. Preparing and enjoying food is an aesthetic experience that nourishes the soul as well as the body. Understanding its origins informs and enhances this experience.

The tomato may be the "poster child" of Italian cuisine, although, in the interest of due respect to this ruby fruit, we need to give credit where it is due.

The Spaniards were responsible for bringing tomatoes to the Mediterranean from South America via the Aztec territories of what is now Mexico. They adapted the name *tomatl* to the Spanish *tomate*. The Italians became familiar with tomatoes on the heels of the *conquistadores* during the Renaissance, at which time they were used as table ornaments. Again, it was the Spanish who, a little later, established the tomato as an edible fruit while they were ruling the Kingdom of Naples. This is appropriate to our tale because the Island of Capri is part of the Metropolitan Area of Naples. So, it can be said with reasonable confidence that tomatoes made their entry in Italian culinary culture there.

The Italian physician and botanist Pietro Andrea Mattioli christened the tomato with the Italian name "pomi d'oro," or golden apples, as both red and yellow tomatoes were available during his lifetime in the sixteenth century. This evolved into today's name for tomato, *pomodoro*, plural *pomodori*.

* * *

While living in Italy, one of my friends invited a small group of us to a farmhouse outside of Rome for the weekend. Now, in my opinion, nothing can touch the magic of putting a handful of people in an isolated house for a few days. Everyone lives their own life and chooses their activities, whether going for walks, shopping for food, feeding the chickens, or napping. Then everyone comes together to prepare dinner, tell stories, and play games. It's an improvised community.

Our host, Elena, had a vegetable garden that was tended by one of her rural neighbors while she was at work in Rome. On the weekend, her neighbor would come to confer about the vegetables and bring her the eggplant and beans he had picked to save them from the small animals that lived on the edge of the nearby forest.

On Friday morning I ventured into the garden, where Elena was busy. She was wearing red wide-legged chinos, a white T-shirt and a straw hat. She showed me her tomato plants, which were tied to stakes amid a mosaic of herbs and flowers. The bed was enclosed with a border of marigolds. Inside that, there was a wider band of oregano that lined the marigolds all around. These two layers of defense protected the tomatoes, under which a host of dandelions grew.

Elena turned to me and said, "The odor of the marigolds keeps the ground animals away, should they get under the wire fence. They also attract predator insects like ladybugs, that eat other pests. The oregano attracts pollinating insects and its strong fragrance acts as a repellent to others."

"What about the dandelions? Are they just weeds?" I asked.

"No, I use them as a groundcover under the tomatoes. They have taproots that keep the soil loose and help circulate nutrients for the tomatoes. And I use the leaves in salads."

Elena's neighbor looked on, approving her handiwork.

He said, "I have mixed flowers with the vegetables in my garden like Signora Elena does, and I have found it works well. There's a lot of activity in the bed, and I think the insects keep one another under control."

The gate opened, and an elegant, mature woman in a silver updo entered.

"Hello, Mamma!" said Elena; and to me, "Let me introduce you to my mother."

Nina, Elena's mother, had gone to the market where she had bought some fresh buffalo mozzarella. "It's for you, *cara*," she said. "I knew you were having guests, and with your tomatoes ripening, I couldn't resist."

Now, Rome is in the Lazio region which, like Campania, the region of Naples and Capri, has a "DOP," or protected designation of origin, for its mozzarella. It was thoughtful of Nina to bring a sought-after and local treat to outsiders like us.

Elena was debating what to do about her mother showing up with a gift of food, and not having much to do once her shopping was done.

"Why don't we all go in and have a coffee?" Elena suggested.

And that's what we did.

Elena continued praising her mother once inside, listing her accomplishments as an academic. Nina was flustered, so she turned away to get the cups and saucers.

"Mamma is going down to Naples next week to give a talk at the University," said Elena.

"More importantly," said Nina, I am going to a reunion of old friends on Capri while I am there. She turned to me and asked, "Have you been to Capri?"

"I was in Naples for a friend's wedding," I said, "and we took the hydrofoil over to the island. I visited the *Grotta Azzurra*, the Blue Grotto, you know, and the usual sights. I loved the cafés and restaurants with their outdoor tables and the winding, narrow streets. You feel the presence of the sea everywhere!"

"Well, you should have seen it in the Fifties," Nina said. "I used to go there with Elena's father before we married. What a scene it was! Everyone was wearing black cropped cigarette pants ..."

"That were later called capris in English," interjected Elena.

"... Which we wore with striped shirts," continued Nina, undeterred, "and sunglasses in the shape of a cat's eye." Nina drew the shape with her finger and thumb in front of her face.

"It was a moment of great conquest for women. The pants were perfect for riding on a scooter, which then was the only sensible way of getting around the island. Although," she added, "the way your father drove wasn't so sensible."

"Where did the Caprese salad come from?" I asked her. "Didn't it emerge around then?"

"Oh, yes," Nina said. "We would go to the Trattoria da Vincenzo for lunch, but we hardly had any money. They served us a tomato and some mozzarella. However, that was *fior di latte*, or cow's milk mozzarella, because they didn't have water buffaloes on Capri!"

That's right: DOP mozzarella comes from water buffaloes.

I asked, "How did water buffaloes get to Italy, anyway?"

"Well," said Nina, "We believe the Romans brought them from the Middle East. They're excellent draught animals, especially in low lying floodplains, and were used originally for plowing and farming. And now, for the best DOP *mozzarella di bufala*."

"So," said Elena, "back to the Caprese salad, Mamma. Tell us more."

Nina put some foamed milk into her espresso, then continued. "We just used a little oil, salt, and pepper, initially. Then people started adding a little bit of wild *rughetta* ..."

"Wait," I said, "is that rucola?"

Elena answered, "Yes, rucola, or arugula; it's called rocket in the U.K."

"And," Nina continued, "oregano grew wild as well, so the trattorias started drying the oregano to crumble over the salad."

"It's so simple," said Elena.

"And so delicious," I added.

"But," Nina said, wagging her finger, "you must use the freshest ingredients to enjoy the Caprese properly. Being there at the right time of year is crucial. Now, the best restaurants and hotels fly the DOP buffalo mozzarella to Capri by helicopter."

"Like Beaujolais?" said our friend Will, who had wandered in to hear the story.

Nina looked at him, disturbed. "Sort of," she said. "Are you French?"

Will, who was English, did not understand the culinary rivalry between Italy and France.

We all laughed.

* * *

My mozzarella isn't flown in by helicopter, but I buy the DOP *mozzarella di bufala,* packaged in its liquid, and the best tomatoes I can find. The local Farmer's Market is the place to go for organic, non-GMO produce. Whatever their source, I put them on my windowsill where they can soak up some sun for a couple of days.

All recipes are fluid over time and geography, although the changes should still respect the essence of the ingredients. Basil is now generally used instead of arugula in the Italian mainstream. Availability may have been the reason, but knowing Italians, I think they may have considered basil more civilized than the bitter-tasting arugula.

It is quite challenging to find basil with the flavor of the Ligurian variety in the northeast U.S. because of our clay soil. So, arugula might be my next garden herb, to use in this dish the way it was once done. That is if the deer leave it alone.

My advice about preparing a Caprese with the best flavor is this:

first, arrange the mozzarella, the tomato slices, and the basil on the serving platter, slightly overlapping the pieces, alternating white, red, and green, like the Italian flag. Then, drizzle the best extra-virgin olive oil you can afford over them. After that, salt just the tomatoes, by gently lifting the mozzarella with a fork where needed. Grind some black peppercorns only over the mozzarella. Finally, crush a piece of dried oregano and sprinkle it on top. The oregano will meet your nostrils first, so think of it as teaser scent, and don't overdo it.

Now, I'm not a wine expert, but I think a California wine works quite well with a Caprese, given the agricultural affinity between Italy and California, not to mention their common roots in Fifties culture. I'm not getting paid for this, but my favorite is Joel Gott unoaked chardonnay from Napa.

Oh, and don't forget to wear your capris and flats. You never know when someone will offer you a ride on their Vespa.

7. Spaghetti alle vongole (Spaghetti with Clams)

My first experience with clams was as an adolescent. One summer, my father decided to buy a dozen. The only problem was that he didn't know how to prepare them, and I found the clams rubbery and gross. Dad must have thought that anything with enough butter on it would be fine.

If you've been to Italy, you will have discovered that the Italians are fond of seafood, which they call *frutti di mare*, or "fruits of the sea." They especially like going to the seaside and dining on the local catch, preferably in the open-air loggia of a restaurant perched on a cliff overlooking the Mediterranean. It's the full experience: all of the senses are engaged.

Of particular interest for this dish are the *arselle* clams, also called *vongole veraci*. They're small, tender and sweet, surpassing any Cape Cod clams for use in pasta. In Italy, the *arselle* clams are found on the Tuscan seacoast, although they are also farmed elsewhere.

During my early years in Milan, I met a woman named Roberta.

She was a graduate of the Art Academy of Brera and had an endless trail of interesting friends and acquaintances, many of which she met at the storefront where she made marbleized paper and objects like albums and boxes and notepads bound and dressed in her handmade paper. Before long, this work evolved into more freeform designs and sculptural objects. Although she was a consummate craftsperson, everything Roberta touched turned into art.

She's tall and bony and in those days had long, wavy strawberry hair. Her clothing draped and flowed, inspired by dance or exotic cultures. She occasionally wore dresses stolen from her mother's collection of 1950's cocktail outfits. Roberta was an "it" girl.

I was intimidated by her, being so uptight and American; and, since I had no money, I always dressed in the frumpiest stuff. Fortunately, her boyfriend and mine were friends, and so we were thrown together. Little by little, I became more assimilated, and she got to know me better. Today, Roberta has come to symbolize and encapsulate that magic period in Milan which, despite the difficulty and loneliness I often experienced, now sits in my memory full of sunny summer evenings with *aperitivos* wherever Roberta held court.

She taught me how to make *spaghetti alle vongole*. We weren't at the seaside at all; we were in Milan where, because it's a wealthy and populous city about two and a half hours away from the coast, you can find good, fresh clams.

There's a tradition of eating clams only during the months with an "r." That, apparently, is because toxins are at a potentially higher level in the warmer months, and shellfish are also spawning during that period. Besides that, it's more likely that clams transported in the summer may be temporarily exposed to high temperatures. These issues have mostly been resolved by farm-raised varieties that are subject to monitoring and controls. So, the "r" rule only holds if you are an amateur digging your own clams or buying directly from independent fishermen.

Roberta is one of the most creative people I've ever met, and during my time in Milan, she loved evoking atmosphere and transporting her guests elsewhere. I suspect she decided to make spaghetti with clams one evening because summer was coming and making this dish would be a way of transporting ourselves to the sea.

Roberta's flat was a three-dimensional expression of her spirit, which was so expansive it was barely contained by the space. She didn't have houseplants; she had a mini-jungle, located in the sweet spot of her living room where the plants fashioned their own architecture and microclimate. Her furniture was comfortable and colorful, the floor covered with patterned rugs. She designed all of the built-in storage with the utmost precision and efficiency. Roberta fashioned some of her handmade paper into lampshades, draping it over custom wire frames. She was also a ceramist, and each of her serving dishes was a casual experiment in her artistic evolution. Her fourth-floor patio was paved with individually painted tiles that she rolled, fired and glazed during her summer retreats to Lake Como. If you visited the bathroom, you'd have found it full of fish-themed objects: hooks, soap dishes, towel designs, framed prints. She bought every fish-thing she found.

When in Milan, we would sit out on her colorful patio before dinner with a glass of wine, the city below hidden by a bamboo hedge that rustled in the breeze.

Many of Roberta's close friends were artists, and little tributes to them existed everywhere: a sculpture, a drawing, a painting; or, something designed by her architect brother.

When we were all still single, Roberta had amazing parties. Her flat was large by big-city standards, and she had opened up two separate rooms to create a single living space. I remember a "paleo fest," and a "tropical fest," not to mention her most completely choreographed party, the Indian fest.

This last party was held some years later after we had all paired off and started having children. Roberta had decided to advance her artistic studies in classical Indian dance and culture at the Dharana Association in Verona. She had always been involved in dance, never having enough ways to express her unrelenting creativity. That, of course, necessitated a makeover of her domestic space with low mattresses, draped fabrics, and cushions, all in the colors of spices. She planned the menu and borrowed her mother's cook to help in the kitchen, while her dog, Dharma, followed her. The men wore turbans and Nehru jackets, while the women wore long-sleeved slit tunics, called *kurta*, over leggings, their wrists adorned with bangles. I had an emerald-green embroidered sari that a friend had brought me from Rajasthan, so I wrapped the six yards of translucent fabric around myself and called a cab. We all got into the role for Roberta, to assist in the realization of her vision. We were a tribe and a scene, thanks to her boundless energy. We chatted in small circles as we always had, enveloped in sitar music and the aroma of curry.

What, you might ask, does this have to do with spaghetti and clams?

Well, these descriptions of Roberta's enchantment with the art and craft and design of everything provides context to her deep understanding of culture and passion for cuisine as well. I wouldn't say that she was a traditionalist in the kitchen, but she understood aesthetics and that there is only one right way to prepare spaghetti and clams.

It's not a meal you can improvise at the last minute.

It starts in the morning, at the fishmongers. The closer you are to the coast, the better. The act of buying the clams at the water's edge sets the stage for the whole aesthetic experience. If you're shopping at the supermarket, you'll have to use your imagination.

If you're not in Italy, try to find the smallest, most tender variety available. If you do prepare spaghetti with clams in the northeastern U.S., I would recommend the small quahog clams called Littlenecks.

Clams are bought alive, and they must be treated well on their last day of existence.

First, you need to discard any clams whose shells are open or broken as these are not safe to eat. The healthy ones can be rinsed with a sprayer and placed into a wide, shallow bowl. They should be just barely covered with cold water sprinkled with coarse salt. The tips of their shells can be poking out of the water. Then, put the bowl in the fridge for a while. This will allow the clams to ingest the water and expel any sand they may contain. That's what they do: they filter seawater.

I usually change the water once, especially if the clams had grit on their shells when purchased. Supermarket clams may already be well-cleaned, but I soak them anyway. It's a ritual. And that's what Roberta does.

Now, when it's time to prepare the meal, don't make the mistake of pouring the bowl out into a colander, as that will just cover the clams with the impurities that were purged by soaking. You have to lift them out by hand or slotted spoon and give them a final rinse. Keep them on a bed of ice or in the refrigerator.

The sauté is made with extra-virgin olive oil, garlic, and small, ripe tomatoes. Keep the burner on low to medium heat while you lightly brown the garlic. You can add some hot pepper flakes or a piece of *peperoncino* if you like it hot, as I do. Then add the tomatoes. I slice them in half and place them flesh side down in the skillet. If you use fresh, ripe tomatoes, then you can cook them as little or as much as you like. If you need to resort to canned diced tomatoes, you'll have to cook them down a little to reduce the liquid.

The timing of the clams with the pasta is tricky: ideally, you'd like them done at the same time. I usually put the pasta into the boiling water right before adding the clams to the sauté. You need to turn the heat up under the skillet when you do. Once it's good and hot, you can turn it down again. You shouldn't use wine, because you'll want to cover the clams and that would prevent evaporation.

The clams will open up when they've had it. They won't open up at the same time, however, so it's a good idea to pull them out as they do so they won't overcook. Some people like to shell half of the clams and leave the other half on the shell in the pasta. If you choose to do so, you can shell the clams that open first and set them aside.

When the clams are nearly all open, wait a little for the stragglers. You may find that a few clams don't open, and these must be discarded as they may not be safe to eat.

Mix the pasta, the sauté and the shelled clams in a large, wide bowl. If the clams on the shell are too hard to manage, pull them out and place them on top of each portion. I prefer mixing everything together for the "buried treasure" effect.

Now, shellfish need to be accompanied by a palate cleanser. Fresh parsley should be added to offset the fishiness. Chop it finely, add it to the dressed pasta and lightly toss it.

If you have guests who aren't crazy about eating clams but have no moral qualms about seafood, I think you'll find that they will enjoy this pasta even if the clams are not in their portion because of the flavor they impart. In this case, I'd leave all the clams on the shell as it's much easier to avoid serving them to your picky eaters.

Remember to place little bowls on the table for the shells and provide ample napkins.

Now that I've shared this with you, I think I'd better call Roberta and see what she's up to.

8. Oranges and Artichokes

During my time in Italy, I loved walking into the greengrocer's at Christmastime: the aroma of oranges filled the space, compensating somewhat for the foggy Milanese December.

In fact, the seasonal rotation of fruits and vegetables in the markets and stores is one of my lasting impressions of that country so tied to the soil, to agriculture, and to food.

To be fair, the best Sicilian blood oranges don't prance onto the culinary stage till later in winter, but the tangy scent of the earlier varieties still makes me think of presents under the Christmas tree.

As a child, I drank orange juice every single day. I couldn't have anything else until I rinsed away the cobwebs of nighttime with its sharp and sunny taste. We usually had frozen concentrate. You opened the cardboard cylinder with its metal caps and dumped it into a Tupperware pitcher; add three cans of water and stir. I had no measure of comparison; we were poor, and it made me happy. Little did I know what joy I'd experience walking down the stone-cold sidewalks of Italy's design capital in the brisk air infused with citrus scents from the open-air crates stacked outside shop windows. It was *meraviglioso*!

Artichokes also remind me of Christmas in Italy. When my son Jacopo was born, we moved from Milan to a part of coastal Tuscany called Versilia. We lived in the hills above Viareggio, in the province of Lucca, overlooking the sea. Every day we strapped Jacopo into his car seat and drove down the switchback roads into Viareggio. We would drive by fields of artichokes, curious about the rows of ferny shrubs with their giant thistle-flower buds. In milder climates, these plants over-winter and are productive for years.

I did have a distant memory of eating artichoke hearts out of small glass jars with my friend Jonathan back in my college days. He would be driving along and, on an impulse, screech to a halt in front of the grocer's. Jonathan would run in and run out again, unscrewing the cap as soon as he got back into the car. As we ate the delicate hearts with our fingers, I thought little about their origin.

That is, until years later, when Piero and I wandered into Sandro's vegetable store. I was carrying Jacopo like a marsupial as we poked through the potatoes when Sandro's activity at the back of the store caught my attention. He was paring an artichoke till there wasn't much left of it. There was a small pile of them on his counter, ready to steam for lunch, so he was happy to show me his technique.

We often see "Globe" artichokes in the U.S., but Sandro offered the more elongated heirloom variety referred to as the *Violetta*, due to its violet tinged-petals.

First, he tore off at least half of the spine-tipped petals, which you might think of as leaves, but you should know that the artichoke is a flower bud. Now, technically these petals are called bracts, but since most people aren't familiar with flower botany, I will refer to them as petals.

You can tell when you've removed enough of them when the tips of the remaining petals are aligned. After Sandro was done, he took a large, sharp knife and chopped the top half of the entire bud in one stroke, holding the stem in his other hand. His next cut was to the stem, which was as long as a carrot. I later learned it could be pared and cooked like one, too. In U.S. supermarkets, we don't generally see artichokes with stems longer than a couple of inches.

Now Sandro held the pared bud, a shadow of its former self, for me to see. Then he cut it in two through the center, exposing the cross-section of its marvelous interior. The inner petals were whorled, going from green to yellow to deep pink; smaller and thinner and more tender as they approached the choke, close to the heart.

Italians call this the *barba*, or beard. The choke, or beard if you prefer, is made of many spiky, fine hair-like petals and looks like a bristle brush. This must be removed with precision because you want to get it all without losing any of the precious, fleshy heart below it. The beard is nasty if you get it in your mouth. It feels extremely dry and is as difficult to swallow as bird feathers (although I have never tried that).

But the name artichoke has nothing to do with that. This plant is native to the western Mediterranean, its origin probably in Sicily or Carthage, the North African city conquered by the Romans. Its original Arabic name was *al-hursufa* which became *alcarchofa* in Spanish and *articiocco* in Northern Italy. Today, Italy is the world's major producer of artichokes, and the proper Italian name is *carciofo*.

But back to removing the beard: with a small, sharp paring knife, Sandro scraped the base of the beard, scooping it out from underneath. It reminded me of cleaning a horse's hoof (this I have tried).

Once all of the nasty beard had been cleaned out, the two halves of the artichoke were ready for cooking. I was amazed at Sandro's skill and the new "vegetable" that was introduced into my life.

Now, the simplest way to prepare artichokes is to steam them till they reach the desired level of tenderness. After they are cool enough to handle, the petals can be peeled off one by one. The bottom part of the petal is fleshy, and this is eaten by scraping it out between your teeth, preferably after dipping it in olive oil. This is a messy though delicious appetizer and a lot of fun for kids. As you make your way, petal by petal, to the heart, the flesh becomes more and more tender; and soon you get to the prize. We have had these for Christmas every year, enjoying them while the roast beef reposed on the counter.

This is a rather delicate dining experience and not the way we would typically serve artichokes to guests. Not everyone wants to get their hands dirty.

As winter wore on, we enjoyed them with mafaldine pasta. This was a special treat because the prep of a half dozen artichokes takes some premeditation. And I learned from an elder relative in Italy to wear gloves when working with the buds. Otherwise, your fingers will get black.

Mafaldine pasta has its own story. Long and flat like a ribbon with ruffled edges, it's similar to very narrow lasagna. It was named (or renamed, some say) after the first-born child of Italy's King Vittorio Emanuele III, the Princess Mafalda. The pasta is also called reginette, or "little queens" for this reason. Princess Mafalda was the daughter of the king who reigned through both World Wars, though the heir to the throne was her younger brother Umberto II, the very last king of Italy.

Mafalda married a German prince who happened to be a member of the Nazi party. After Italy had surrendered to the Allies but before Germany was defeated, Mafalda was arrested by the Gestapo and sent to Buchenwald, where she died of injuries during a nearby Allied bombing. Adolph Hitler and Joseph Goebbels never liked her, although her husband was merely put under house arrest by the Germans, brought into custody by the British, and later released. The advantages of being a male royal, I guess.

Thankfully, Princess Mafalda has been immortalized by this pasta, and it's one of the reasons I like to use *mafaldine* with artichokes.

This is how I make *mafaldine ai carciofi*. You already know how to prepare the artichokes, which is the majority of the work. Now you can put the water on for the pasta and get to work on the sauté. Place the artichokes halves flat side down on a cutting board and slice into one-quarter inch pieces. On low-medium heat, brown a couple of garlic cloves in extra-virgin olive oil. Then add the chopped artichokes. I usually separate the more tender parts like the heart and add them a few minutes later. If you're using the stems, make sure they're pared and sliced. They can go in right away. Stir the sauté for a few minutes and deglaze with some white wine when necessary.

I prefer cooking at lower temperatures with the skillet covered. If you like fast stir-fry cooking, you must peel the artichokes further to eliminate all but the tenderest petals: you should be able to bite a piece off while they're raw.

Slower cooking really brings out the very particular flavor of the artichokes. Remember that it is a bud and must be treated delicately. Let them simmer and soften a little before you put the pasta into the salted, boiling water.

If you need to add liquid to the sauté, scoop some water from the pasta pot. If there's too much liquid, uncover it and let it evaporate before the pasta is ready.

Empty the skillet into the serving bowl, drain the *mafaldine*, and run the pasta around the skillet to clean it. Always add a little bit of raw olive oil to the pasta before mixing it thoroughly. This gives the dish a subtle aroma. Top it off with some freshly grated parmigiano cheese. This can be sprinkled on individually if you have vegan guests.

I know that Americans typically like to stuff artichokes, although I think the "proper death" of an artichoke bud is one that allows it to stand alone (except for the garlic; I mean, are you kidding?). The ruffled edges of the mafaldine capture the pieces of artichoke nicely, and if the pasta and the sauté are cooked just right, the textural combination will be sublime.

So, you might ask, where do the oranges fit in? We like to follow *mafaldine ai carciofi* with a salad of Sicilian blood oranges and raw fennel, both of which are available in winter. The peeled oranges and the fennel are both sliced into thin discs and dressed only with extra-virgin olive oil, salt, and freshly ground black pepper. For a midday meal, this combination is hard to beat.

Italy is far and away the world's most important producer of artichokes, and April is actually the peak season. However, due to the variations of climate throughout Italy, and the demand for artichokes, summer is really the only truly "off" season, when late spring and summer vegetables gain prominence. So, if you decide to travel to Italy in the spring, you will find a good number of artichoke festivals, especially in central and southern Italy.

For me, oranges and artichokes will always be the delights that get me through the winter.

9. Melanzane con la rucola (Eggplant with Arugula)

I was born in the northeast of the United States and never had much contact with eggplant while growing up. When I was in college, the earthy ecological types, often vegetarians, would prepare ratatouille, a French dish that people would either misspell or mispronounce, depending on whether they encountered the word written or spoken first.

Then there was Eggplant Parmigiano.

I never really liked it, because the eggplant always seemed to be undercooked. For this dish, it is breaded and browned in the skillet before layering it with the other ingredients such as sauce and cheese and baking it in the oven. I was unimpressed. These dishes that included eggplant in a medley seemed to be avoiding the naked truth: that eggplant by itself just wasn't tasty. Its sponginess makes this vegetable the perfect medium to soak up whatever else is in the pot.

Living in Italy provided me with many opportunities, one of which was learning how to love eggplant. Did you know that botanically speaking, eggplant are berries? This becomes evident when you observe the plant while the fruit is developing. They definitely dangle.

Raw eggplant is inedible. It's very bitter, and its skin is like leather. Being a member of the nightshade family, eggplant naturally has some "dark" characteristics: it contains nicotinoid alkaloids. These alkaloids protect the fruit from pests while it's ripening. As you may imagine, eggplant is related to tobacco, but also to potatoes, tomatoes, and peppers.

Italians have a rule that you should never eat something green if it will in time turn another color. That means, generally, no green tomatoes or green peppers. Eggplant, if not fully ripened, will have a green edge inside the skin. The problem is that food distribution has encouraged shipping unripe fruit and vegetables, so you should buy the types you like regularly, preferably in season, and set them on your kitchen windowsill or in hanging baskets for a few days.

The best solution is to cultivate your own eggplant if you are fortunate enough to live where there is a long growing season. Or, as in my case, take advantage of your neighbor's bounty.

When Piero and I left Tuscany to be closer to Milan, we settled on a small town that was an hour's drive west of the city, in the vicinity of Lago Maggiore. It was a small rural community. There was an older and very kind man named Imo who lived across the road. His nephew Ugo lived next door. Ugo didn't have any land to speak of, so he planted and maintained an ample vegetable garden at Imo's house, sharing the produce with him.

Ugo was a curious guy. He was robust, bearded and bespectacled. He wore tunics and sandals and spoke English like a colonial East

Indian. His home was filled with Indian artifacts like statues of Ganesh and the Buddha. His office was full of fountain pens and exotic trinkets. Ugo traveled to India every winter to buy things to sell at the markets in Italy in the summertime. After years of trading objects of small value, he zeroed in on Victorian-era nautical instruments found on the subcontinent, moved into a restored farmhouse and populated his new office with antique globes, sextants, and compasses. But he still grew his own vegetables. Have land, will cultivate: that's the Italian motto. In a way, eggplant, which goes by the name of brinjal in India, traveled between Asia and Italy just like Ugo did.

One year, Ugo had more eggplant than he and Imo could possibly consume. We had just begun our friendship and would often see Ugo walking along from the window of our small kitchen. During this particular summer, he would stop by the window and offer me some eggplant. I took it, of course, not knowing what else to do, but I needed to find some use for it as it began to appear on my windowsill every day whether I was home or not. Thus began my education in the proper care of this berry-fruit that we call a vegetable.

The first thing you need to do with ripe eggplant is to make it sweat. You have to cut it into quarter-inch discs and lay it out, sprinkling it with coarse sea salt. After a half hour or so, moisture will bead up on the slices. Now you can rinse and cook the eggplant.

Ugo gave me more than Piero and I could eat, so I developed a technique of rapid-pickling the eggplant. For this preparation, I would slice the eggplant even thinner. I'd boil water with vinegar in it, drop the sweated slices into the pot for a couple of minutes, a few at a time, then carefully take them out and set them aside. Once they had cooled, I layered them with extra-virgin olive oil, garlic, fresh basil, and *peperoncino*. I put this assemblage into the fridge, so it was ready to eat any time over the following days.

Piero and I had some new friends who were vegetarians, and I was a beginner at making dinner for people with dietary restrictions. Now, you may be familiar with the classic summer plate of bresaola with arugula and shaved parmigiano. Bresaola is raw, cured beef like *carpaccio*, so that wouldn't work, though I decided to use that dish as my template, and substituted the "pickled" eggplant for the bresaola.

I simply made a bed of arugula on each plate and topped it with the eggplant and shaved parmigiano. We served this after a simple pasta dish, and it was a big hit.

Italians have an orthodox culinary culture, so it's fun to come up with something they hadn't thought of, but which fits in with their canon. It looked familiar and contained a simple array of ingredients.

The next summer, when Piero and I were on the island of Menorca, off the Catalonian coast of Spain, we once again found ourselves amid an abundant eggplant crop. By that time, I had devised another method of speeding up the whole prep process, as I generally cook like I am extinguishing a fire. This was my skillet technique. I cut the eggplant into discs, then quartered the discs and tossed them into a garlic and olive oil sauté. Then, I sprinkled it with salt, cranked up the heat, and covered the skillet to force-sweat the eggplant. After about ten minutes, I removed the cover and allowed the moisture to evaporate. For this approach, you need to be careful about the amount of salt you use, although I have generally found that it is about what I would use in the sauce anyway. You can always reduce the salt added to the pasta water to compensate. Now tomatoes could be added to the skillet.

But I still hadn't found the ideal technique, one that would make me really love eggplant. Until I met Roberto, who did. Now Piero would eat anything that was placed in front of him and rave about it. He was so grateful to have things prepared for him and so utterly incapable of doing it for himself. Roberto, on the other hand, is very particular about his eggplant.

His technique is straightforward: select small, firm fruit in season and make sure it's ripe; sweat the sliced pieces and rinse off the bitter fluid and salt; lay the eggplant on an oven sheet and brush it with extra-virgin olive oil; then, roast the living hell out of it. When it's done, it will be browned, and the moisture content in the slices will be minimal.

Roberto makes penne pasta with roasted eggplant. Just toss it with some raw olive oil.

From this, I've learned that roasted eggplant can be used in any dish calling for it, including ratatouille. In this case, the eggplant doesn't act like a sponge for the liquid but instead adds a bit of texture and smokiness to the sauce.

And it goes without saying that roasted eggplant is sublime on a bed of arugula, drizzled with a little olive oil, a squeeze of lemon, and topped with shaved parmigiano.

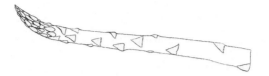

10. Asparagus risotto

One of the advantages of living in the northern Italian city of Milan is its location relative to many beautiful places: in a few hours or less, you can reach France, Switzerland, or the beautiful Dolomite mountains. If you drive from Milan due east towards Venice and turn left at Verona, you'll be heading north into the alpine region. It's called Alto Adige but is also referred to as the South Tyrol. The Tyrolean region straddles the Austrian border and the South, or *Südtirol*, now part of Italy, was under Austrian rule until the end of World War I. The Austrian Empire under the Habsburgs once held the Lombard and Venetian regions as well, but these had already been surrendered to Italy during its unification in the nineteenth century. The Italian Südtirol is nestled between Switzerland and Austria and shares many characteristics, including landscape and culture, with those countries. Mountain people are mountain people everywhere.

The Milanese are sometimes wistful about the days when Lombardy was under Austria rather than in its current predicament as the bootstrap of the Italian economy. Indeed, the people of Italy's financial capital sometimes seem more Mittel-European than Italian. It's quite common to see articles of Tyrolean clothing like boiled wool jackets with stamped metal buttons, or Loden capes and overcoats in their classic olive color, during the Milanese winter. Though Milan is a leading fashion capital worldwide, the Milanese themselves have a strict dress code that emphasizes quality of materials over trendiness.

Given the cultural significance of the South Tyrol to my adopted city, I was pleased when my husband Piero suggested a trip there, a three-and-a-half hour's drive from Milan.

The alpine region was a surprise for me as I hadn't realized there was a whole chunk of Italy that resembled Austria, where many of the people spoke German or a dialect called Ladin. There you can pick blueberries and eat Wienerschnitzel, a precursor to the famed Milanese cutlet.

The city of Bolzano is a commercial hub, and its covered sidewalks allow browsing in comfort among its beautiful shops offering woolen clothing with horn buttons and mountain hats with feathers and pins. Festivals in this city's main square feature men in *lederhosen* slapping and stomping in their traditional dance called the *Schuhplattler*. If you visit in winter, you should, however, beware of an invitation by the locals to go "cross-country" skiing: their version entails a straight-up vertical ascent followed by a death-defying downhill, dodging trees on narrow trails. It's an initiation of sorts.

Piero had a German grandmother who used to enjoy visiting the small South Tyrolese city of Merano. Because of his memories of this spa town nestled in one of the many alpine valleys of the region, we decided to travel there together in springtime. I experienced my first Asparagus Festival during that trip.

Merano is situated in a broad basin opening to the south, surrounded by the majestic Dolomite mountains. The streams are stony and lively, and everything seems fresh and clean. As soon as the weather permits, flower pots line the streets and hang from the window sills of the blocky, chalet-style buildings stuccoed white with brown trim. There isn't a lot happening in this town, although it's a great place to recover from big city life by hiking, visiting the spa resorts, eating, and sleeping. Our visit included a shopping trip to Bolzano, where we couldn't resist buying a pair of *lederhosen* for Jacopo, who was two years old at the time.

The agricultural pursuits in and around Merano include the cultivation of apples and cool-weather grapes used to make the wines for which the region is known.

At the time of our visit, however, it was asparagus season. Now, asparagus is well-appreciated throughout Italy, but its appearance in the more northern localities is cause for celebration: it's the vegetable that heralds the arrival of spring. Every restaurant along our route boasted asparagus soup, pasta with asparagus, asparagus with eggs, and so on.

The part of the asparagus plant that we eat is the shoot. These emerge from the base or crown, which is planted in shallow trenches and covered in loose, nutrient-rich soil. Further north, in Germany, asparagus is blanched by keeping the emerging shoots buried. This prevents them from turning green. In Italy, asparagus is typically green with violet shading on the lateral scales and tips.

Growing asparagus requires some patience because it takes a couple of years before you can expect a decent crop. Once you succeed, however, the plants produce for some years. Asparagus beds must be well-tended and weed-free because this plant is a fussy aristocrat among vegetables.

The trend these days is to sell asparagus throughout the year. This is a pity because it takes away the excitement of spring's arrival and the appreciation of the beautiful spears that are locally grown and in season. I'm a picky spear picker, though I limit my harvesting to the grocery store. When the season begins, you will know it. The store crates are in the front line, and the asparagus stands bundled in trays with their lower stalks in water. In milder climates, this could be March, though April is more typical for temperate regions.

So, the first thing you need to do is wait for this magic moment. Then, look for spears whose tips are closed tight and undamaged. If they have loosened, that means they were on the verge of developing their lacy fronds, the vegetation necessary to feed the plant for the following year. At that point, however, the shoots will have toughened up, and they are past their prime.

The bottoms of the spears are white, and these should be kept moist. Make sure the bundle you choose has its feet in water. If you're lucky enough to have your own asparagus plants, you will keep the spears standing upright in a little water until you're ready to prepare them.

Asparagus spears may be sandy, so they need to be gently rinsed with a sprayer. Then, holding the spear in both hands, bend it, and it will snap, separating the tender portion from the tougher base. Some people say there's no point in doing this because you can just cut the spears. I prefer the snapping ritual, and in my memory, this is one of the tasks my little children loved doing to help in the kitchen. The sound also creates a sense of anticipation.

After snapping, you'll discard about one-quarter of the spear, the white portion, to compost or for making broth. The usable part of the spear can be prepared whole, although for this asparagus risotto recipe, it should be cut on the diagonal in pieces about the length of the tip. The tips should be set apart because they require less cooking time.

The ideal companion for asparagus in this dish is the shallot. It has a more delicate flavor than onion and is, therefore, a better supporting actor, allowing the asparagus to shine. The herb I prefer is tarragon, which is also used in Béarnaise sauce with shallots. If you have any garden space, you should grow your own herbs as they require very little work. If you plant tarragon, make sure it's the French variety, as that is the best for cooking, and give it some room to spread.

The sauté is beginning to feel more French than Italian, so you may not be surprised when I suggest that butter should be used instead of olive oil. Once again, it is the concept of a "proper death" that the Italians subscribe to, and most people will agree that butter is the appropriate grave for shallots. However, if you have dietary restrictions or beliefs, you can substitute the butter with extra-virgin olive oil.

The shallot should be finely sliced but not minced. I don't like minced anything because it reminds me of over-prepared food without texture. The heat should be slow and steady to avoid burning the butter, so if you don't have a skillet with a thick bottom, you will need to be vigilant. The tarragon, whether you prefer sprigs or crumbled leaves, should be added now so that the butter will be infused with its anise-like flavor.

Once the shallots are tender and clear, you'll be adding the carnaroli or arborio rice. Stir it with a wooden spatula so it can evenly toast in the sauté. You want the rice to harden on the outside so that it will be more resistant to overcooking. The most common error I've seen in the U.S. is overcooking; risotto should be *al dente*. Keep the wine you'll be serving with the risotto handy to deglaze the skillet as needed.

At this point, the grains of rice have toughened on the outside, and it's time to add the broth. I suggested earlier that the bottoms of the asparagus stalks can be used for this. If you plan to do that, you'll have to prep the asparagus well ahead of time as the broth should simmer for a couple of hours.

Making broth is an adventure of its own. If you have the opportunity to save discarded parts of raw vegetables, you can make broth every week and store it for use in risottos and soups. For some dishes, you may want to select which vegetables go into the broth. Some chefs also use fruit. For this risotto, the best ingredients are the asparagus stalk bottoms, leftover rinds of parmigiano cheese, and celery. These are all rather delicate flavors that stand aside so that the asparagus can take the lead. You may want to experiment. Both variety and hierarchy should be considered.

When we make boiled rice, we generally add two cups of water for every cup of rice right away. For risotto, the broth is added a little at a time, so you'll have to get comfortable in front of the stove. That might mean you need a glass of Gewürztraminer, a fruity white wine that comes from cooler grape-growing regions like Alto Adige. Müller-Thurgau is another Italian-grown variety that's a little drier. If you don't have travel memories to evoke as I do, you could also try a dry Riesling from the Finger Lakes Region of New York.

If you don't drink, a glass of sparkling grape juice will be an excellent substitute.

But we should get back to the risotto!

There are different approaches to cooking the asparagus. The simplest is by adding it to the risotto. This will require some judgment about cooking time to get the asparagus to the desired tenderness, but it should be after you start adding the broth to the rice. Remember to add the tips later. Another alternative is to steam the asparagus without cooking it entirely and fold it into the risotto near the end. I would only do this if the broth were made with asparagus scraps because some flavor will be lost. Finally, you could broil the spears if you want an earthier taste. In this case, it would be cooked ahead of time, cut afterward, and added when the risotto is almost done.

I prefer adding the asparagus to the risotto because, after a little practice, it's not hard to tell how much time you'll need to get the asparagus where you want it. You can regulate heat and broth as needed as long as you don't overcook the rice.

The last step is to add parmigiano cheese to the risotto in the skillet and plate it right away.

Every time I make asparagus risotto, I think of our trip to the mountains of the South Tyrol where asparagus was featured in every version on every menu, and little Jacopo bouncing in his *lederhosen*.

With every arrival of spring, there is new hope and new life.

11. Carrot Pasta

In Italy there is a rule about where to spend the holidays: *Natale con i tuoi e Pasqua con chi vuoi,* which means, "Christmas with your family and Easter with whomever you like." And I must admit that Easter doesn't hold much interest for a recovering Catholic like me with no kids around.

Our children, thankfully, still find joy in the indulgences of this holiday, and have never refused an Easter basket, whatever its contents.

Easter is nothing like Christmas with its magic and lights and paper and bows. Still, it's a celebration of life represented by bunnies and chicks and crocuses peeking from emerging grass, regardless of your beliefs. It represents the triumph of life over death.

When I was a child, I didn't consider the meaning of Easter beyond getting a new hat, dress, and shoes to wear to church. Once I became a mother myself, I was able to appreciate the pain my mother must have felt in trying to buy us some new things on a small budget.

She eventually taught me how to use the sewing machine so that I could make my own dress.

But getting up Easter morning was nonetheless a wonder. The day before, a Saturday of course, we colored the boiled eggs that my mother had set on our long kitchen table. We fought over the cups of color and the wire egg holder, drawing with wax crayons then dipping into one color and the next in a contest of originality. We each had an egg with our name on it, in addition to some wildcard eggs and, most importantly, the Golden Egg. This would garner the biggest prize during the hunt on Easter morning.

We would get out of bed quite early and go down to the dining room where the reed baskets, bedded with gaudy colored grass and full of chocolates and candy, were mysteriously wrapped in translucent cellophane. Now, this is a touch I attribute to my mother. The pink or yellow "see-through" wrapping impeded us from tearing them open without consent, yet we were able to discern the identity of most of their contents and speculate about others. And possibly sneak a few fingers inside.

Mom made a sweet, braided Easter bread that had colored eggs embedded in it. When our father was ready, we would have our breakfast, but not before he sprinkled the table with holy water that he had obtained from our parish priest. He would stand at the head of the table with his eyes half closed, while we rolled our own eyes and looked at one another as if to say, "oh, brother!" the way Catholic school kids do when subjected to any religious ceremony.

After we had our breakfast we were allowed to open our baskets.

No, that's not really true; we had already lobbied to have a crack at them before we ate.

The Easter egg hunt was next, and the prizes of shiny half-dollars fresh from the bank went to whoever found the Golden Egg as well as the most eggs. Then our mother would realize that we hadn't made a proper inventory and could only hope that we hadn't left any eggs undiscovered to become petrified behind the drapes, or worse. We often had the hunt indoors, especially if Easter was early, due to muddy conditions.

These memories explain why I can't entirely give up on Easter. The innocent joy of children is a life-saver for adults and, fortunately, our grown kids have not lost the connection to their childhood selves. But as they have grown, the Easter dinner menu has become more controversial.

Some families have the same kind of meal at Easter that they enjoy at Christmas: a beef roast, a turkey, or a ham. In Italy, lamb is considered the traditional main course though I've never prepared a roast lamb myself. We used to have the small chops called lollipops because they appealed to my kids when they were young. However, after I had returned to the States and Roberto and I merged our families, Jacopo, Pinuccia, and now Roxy were old enough to have their say in our Easter menu.

And none of them wanted anything to do with eating a baby lamb in any form. Fair enough; after all, Easter is the feast of life and, despite the role of death in the Christian story of rebirth, we decided it was time to go vegetarian.

The problem became one of choosing the vegetable that could rise to the symbolic role of the Easter story. I looked around, and there it was, sitting on a small plate left for the Easter Bunny: a slender carrot that was missing a single bite.

Now, in early spring we still depend on root vegetables to carry us through till spinach and asparagus and artichokes arrive, so the carrot was a practical choice. But on further consideration, I realized its more profound appropriateness. First, the carrot has great symbolic value: it has to go down into the ground before it can come up again, a resurrection of sorts. And secondly, carrots were food for bunnies and bunnies are cute.

The next problem was determining how a dish based on carrots could be significant enough to celebrate this rite of spring. For an Italian, the first thing that comes to mind is pasta.

By now you get that Italians adhere to certain rules about the compatibility of ingredients and the role of each in creating a symphony of flavor. I had to take some liberties with this dish, although I believed that my understanding of the "basic template" would help me to create a simple recipe that even the most orthodox of Italian culinary mavens would accept.

One of the rules requires knowledge of the vegetable, which

allows you good judgment in its selection. The quality of ingredients is king.

Carrots should be planted in well-drained, sandy soil. When these roots run into obstacles underground, they become distorted. Straight carrots mean they were grown in the sandy soil they like.

When you slice a carrot, you'll notice that it has an outer, pulpy area called the cortex, surrounding a core that's slightly different in color. The best carrots have a smaller core relative to the cortex.

To protect carrots from pests in the garden, strongly scented plants like chives, scallions or shallots are perfect companions. This makes them a natural choice to add to this dish. I prefer shallots for their delicate flavor since onions would be too harsh or require too much cooking time.

You'll need an aromatic herb, of course. The carrot, once used only for its leaves and seeds, has botanical relatives that include parsley, cilantro, fennel, anise, and dill. Anise is used to make black jellybeans, which made me consider it for this Easter dish, but then I thought it might be it too suggestive of candy. I decided on tarragon, which is delicately reminiscent of anise without the strong association with sweets or spirits.

I've mentioned my preference for butter in the shallot sauté, and that's why I begin with thinly sliced shallots in butter on low heat. While that's cooking, I put a pot of water on for the pasta. Then I shred the carrots with the large holes of a cheese grater. I've tried using a food processor, but it tends to make a pulp, which isn't the right texture. I'll use *penne rigate* for this, and the hand-shredded carrot adheres to this type of pasta well.

When the shallot sauté is soft and clear, I add the tarragon and move it around to moisten. I prefer dried, ground leaves for this recipe. Fresh tarragon can be crushed with a mortar and pestle after stripping the leaves from the twigs. Then, add the carrots. I usually use one carrot per person, plus one for the Easter bunny.

Good carrots should be moist when shredded, so I cover the sauté to create steam. This makes all of the flavors circulate. Your job now is to regulate the amount of liquid so the carrots don't dry out. You can scoop some water from the pot where the pasta is now cooking, a couple of tablespoons at a time. If you need to reduce the moisture level, a question of personal taste, just remove the cover of the skillet and keep stirring. Ask if someone is willing to grate some parmigiano cheese while you're doing this. Finally, sprinkle a tiny amount of nutmeg, maybe a quarter of a teaspoon, to enrich the bouquet.

Once the pasta is cooked *al dente*, place the penne in a large bowl and add the contents of the skillet to it. Now, you need to add a knob of butter to the mixture. In Italian, this is called *mantecare*, which means to use a fat like butter or cream to smooth and fuse the ingredients. It's often done for risotto but is ideally suited to this pasta dish as well.

Now all you need to do is serve this to your family and pass around the parmigiano.

Our daughters, in particular, love this dish. Roxy has proudly made this one of the critical recipes in her pasta repertoire. In fact, I was so pleased when she texted me one evening urgently asking for the recipe for a dinner party she was preparing. She has had a resurrection of her own.

My carrot pasta, while entirely made in the U.S.A., wouldn't have been possible without the approach to cooking that I learned while living in Italy. I'm looking forward to preparing it for my friends the next time I'm there. If they decide to spend Easter with me, we'll see what they think!

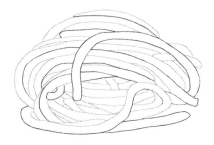

12. La "spaghettata"

It was dark and all the stores were closed when we arrived at Emanuela's restored farmhouse in the country outside of Milan. We both had children to settle into bed, which we did, though my own house was only a few kilometers away. Pinuccia was in her portable crib in the living room, and Jacopo was curled up on the couch.

We went into the kitchen to see what we could rustle up for our dinner. The only thing in the fridge was a clove of garlic and a half-empty bottle of white wine.

"Oh, we have wine!" said Emanuela. And she poured us each a glass.

I sat at the kitchen table as she pulled a few things out of the cupboards: a box of spaghetti, a canister of breadcrumbs, and some dried herbs. There was rosemary, oregano, and sage that she had harvested from a small, south-facing bed outside of the kitchen, in the small garden between her house and the stucco-and-brick barn.

Emanuela was the attractive, though not beautiful, daughter of a countess and a stockbroker. She was confident, hard-edged even, and looked for amusement from the company she kept. Emanuela went to Milan when necessary but was more comfortable walking her country property in her rubber boots, the dogs by her side. She once invited me to go riding. Her mother had a kennel and stables near a large tract of field and forest that was used for fox hunting. We rode across an open area towards the woods, led by a groom on his mount, then proceeded to tear through the trees on a narrow path. I started to worry when my baseball cap was knocked off by the branch of a tree.

That's when Emanuela turned around and said, "Keep your butt out of the saddle!"

Oh.

Anyway, I made it out without falling off my horse, and I'm still very proud of that fact today.

Back at the worn oak table in her kitchen, while her aged golden retriever slept underneath, I watched the intrepid Emanuela prepare something from nothing.

She put on a pot of water for the spaghetti, then she toasted the single garlic clove in some extra-virgin olive oil. Of course, there was always some olive oil in the house. Then she crushed the dried herbs, mixed them with a generous handful of breadcrumbs, and added this to the garlic and oil in the skillet on low heat. Emanuela stirred this with a wooden spoon, blending the flavors and the oil, and that was it.

The pasta was cooked to perfection, drained and emptied into the skillet to mix.

I was undoubtedly hungry at the time, but I remember thinking that nothing had ever tasted so good. It was like having leftover dressing from a Thanksgiving turkey. Pasta with breadcrumbs is like a painting of a polar bear in a snowstorm: white on white, but it works.

A quick pasta dish thrown together with whatever is in the kitchen is called a *spaghettata*. There is no good way to translate this into English. Spaghetti is a common type of pasta, so Italians looking for something to eat might say, "Shall we make a couple of spaghetti?" Or, "How about a *spaghettata*?" I think you get the idea.

On another occasion, my friend Gilberto, son of a restaurateur, whipped up an *aglio, olio e peperoncino*, the simple pasta tossed with a sauté of oil, garlic, and hot pepper. He made it for us one night because he had just been down south and had brought back these beautiful dried hot peppers. Nobody felt like cooking, but we were hungry. He slit the *peperoncini* and put them into the skillet to sauté whole with a few cloves of garlic and extra-virgin olive oil. He later fished the big pieces out to save us.

And then there was my friend Angela, whose children would balk at anything they were served. I would prepare a pasta sauce that my children loved, and Angela would walk over to me at the stove and ask if I could make some *pasta in bianco*, or "white" pasta, for her kids. Basically, this meant plain pasta. When the pot was drained, I'd set aside a small amount of spaghetti without the sauce and dress it with butter and grated cheese. It's the Italian version of mac & cheese, and a go-to meal for Italian kids who are hard to please. I sometimes thought this was a way for their mothers to assure their children would not become attached to anyone's cooking but their own. To be honest, it's good, and a great dish for someone who is ill or has tummy troubles.

In Rome, there's a traditional pasta dish called *cacio e pepe*, which means "cheese and pepper," and while there are as many variations as there are cooks, it's made with butter, pecorino romano cheese, and freshly ground black pepper. I mean, this is so easy, you only need to grate the cheese and grind the pepper!

Now, to make this, you just cook some form of long pasta like thin spaghetti, my favorite. While it's in the pot, melt a knob of unsalted butter in a large skillet, then add some freshly ground black pepper. You could also toast whole peppercorns in the dry skillet before crushing them, in which case you'd need to use a mortar and pestle.

Drain the pasta about two minutes before it's done, reserving some of the water and setting it aside. Transfer the spaghetti into the skillet with the melted butter and pepper. Add a small amount of the cooking water to the mixture right away and stir the pasta. You have to use your judgment about how much liquid, depending on the amount of pasta you've made. I'd start out with a half cup for a pound of pasta and add as needed. You don't want it to be soupy or risk overcooking the spaghetti because you've added too much water. While you're mixing the pasta in the skillet, sprinkle the pecorino cheese generously. Some prefer to add the cheese after the skillet has been removed from the heat.

You'll find recipes for *cacio e pepe* that use parmigiano cheese and pecorino together. That is entirely up to you. I think what an Italian cook would do is rummage around in the fridge and use whatever sort of hard cheese happens to be there. Pecorino romano is the signature cheese, and if I had to choose a second cheese, I think I'd use *ricotta salata*, an aged, firm type of ricotta, and crumble it on the pasta before serving.

I'm always amazed by the pasta offered at many restaurants in the States: they have everything on it but the kitchen sink. Pasta is treated like a pizza, and the type of pasta used is entirely interchangeable: you can have the same sauce on angel hair, penne, or linguine. You'll see peppers and chicken and tomatoes and onions piled on top of a bed of twice-cooked pasta that would be better substituted with a simple piece of bread.

The point I'm trying to make is that the ingredients, the process, and even the traditions are essential to everyday Italian cooking. The recipes I've mentioned, while prepared almost with eyes closed, are emblematic of an approach based on simplicity and intuition. Therein lies the beauty of a *spaghettata*.

First, you have to use good quality pasta made from durum wheat semolina. I use De Cecco, but there are other good brands. Good dried pasta "holds its cooking," which means it should be *al dente* if you follow the recommended cooking time. Some inferior types will go from undercooked to overcooked without ever hitting that sweet spot.

Unfortunately, this is something you'll have to learn through experience. Even if you buy good pasta and respect the timing, there are other factors to consider.

Next, you should use a generous pot of water. You don't want the pasta to be crowded. If your water quality isn't great, consider getting a tap filter. An eight-quart pot will work for a box of pasta. I use a larger one when we have guests.

You must salt the water before putting in the pasta. Do this once the water is at a rolling boil. I use coarse sea salt, a small handful for a pound of pasta. If you're serious about making great pasta, I recommend focusing on the basics first. Make plain pasta, and just add a little fresh extra-virgin olive oil to it when it's ready. This will allow you to judge the quality of the pasta, the amount of salt added, and the proper cooking time. It should be good like this, just like a yummy piece of buttered bread.

When you add cheese, you're adding salt, so that's the next thing to test. Parmigiano is our go-to cheese, and we always use it freshly grated. Another favorite cheese for grating is pecorino romano, which is sharper and saltier. It's worth shopping around for the best quality cheese, even if it means using less. If there's an Italian specialty store or a public market in your area, you can compare their products with those at your favorite supermarket.

Once you've mastered the basics, you can start to have fun adding ingredients each time. Think of them as "essences." What are your favorites? You can try garlic, herbs, capers, anchovies, grated truffle, finely-chopped roasted vegetables: you name it!

Making a *spaghettata* is all about improvisation.

It's also about sharing a meal with friends and family and enjoying life.

Buon appetito!

Afterward

I hope that you've enjoyed these stories and have understood their intention: to introduce you to the significance of food as a cultural expression, to encourage curiosity about the precious ingredients used, and to appreciate the importance of eating with our loved ones and friends, a source of beautiful memories and rich experience. Now, it is up to you to create your own stories of food and life.

If you liked these stories, I welcome your review on the platform of your choice. And you might want to check out my novels, "Meet Me in Milano," and "Blue Sky with Clouds," which, along with their engaging tales, feature more content about Italian food culture.

About the Author

Mariuccia Milla is an "Ameritalian" writer, designer, and critic.

Mariuccia has spent half of her adult life in Italy and half in the Finger Lakes region of New York State.

Her background in landscape architecture has led her to draw setting and landscape into her stories as influential factors in the dynamics among her characters. The ritual of preparing food and eating with loved ones is another important theme in her books.

Her first work, "Meet Me in Milano," is about a young American woman who sets out for escape, adventure, and self-discovery in Milan, Italy's creative capital. "Blue Sky with Clouds" explores similar themes with two middle-aged Italian women who find themselves in the Finger Lakes Region of New York. Both novels are an exploration of the influence that very diverse people have on one another when they become part of an improvised community in a place with a personality all its own.

You can find Mariuccia Milla at www.mariucciamilla.com and on Facebook and Instagram @mariumilla.

If you enjoyed this book, please consider posting a review on the platform of your choice.

Arrivederci!

Made in the USA
Middletown, DE
17 April 2019